Creepy UFOs

Walt Brody

Lerner Publications • Minneapolis

Lerner Publications Company
An imprint of Lerner Publishing Group, Inc.
241 First Avenue North
Minneapolis, MN 55401 USA

For reading levels and more information, look up this title at www.lernerbooks.com.

Main body text set in Billy Infant regular.
Typeface provided by SparkType.

Photo Editor: Rebecca Higgins

Library of Congress Cataloging-in-Publication Data

Names: Brody, Walt, 1978- author.
Title: Creepy UFOs / Walt Brody.
Description: Minneapolis : Lerner Publications, [2021] | Series: Lightning bolt books. Spooked | Includes bibliographical references and index. | Audience: Ages 6-9 | Audience: Grades K-1 | Summary: "Tales of alien abductions and extraterrestrial sightings have haunted us over the years. But how much is the truth? Simultaneously creepy, fascinating, and kid-friendly, this book explores the truth behind the myths—but beware: discover at your own risk!"— Provided by publisher.
Identifiers: LCCN 2019044207 (print) | LCCN 2019044208 (ebook) | ISBN 9781541596894 (library binding) | ISBN 9781728400471 (ebook)
Subjects: LCSH: Unidentified flying objects—Sightings and encounters—Juvenile literature. | Extraterrestrial beings—Juvenile literature.
Classification: LCC TL789.2 .B757 2021 (print) | LCC TL789.2 (ebook) | DDC 001.942—dc23

LC record available at https://lccn.loc.gov/2019044207
LC ebook record available at https://lccn.loc.gov/2019044208

Manufactured in the United States of America
1-47795-48235-11/22/2019

Table of Contents

What Is a UFO?

On July 14, 2001, a crowd stopped on a New Jersey highway. They watched strange lights in the sky. Were the lights an alien spaceship?

In 1953, the US Air Force called these strange things UFOs, or unidentified flying objects. Many people think UFOs are alien spaceships.

Some people say they have seen an alien spaceship. Some even say they have been aboard one.

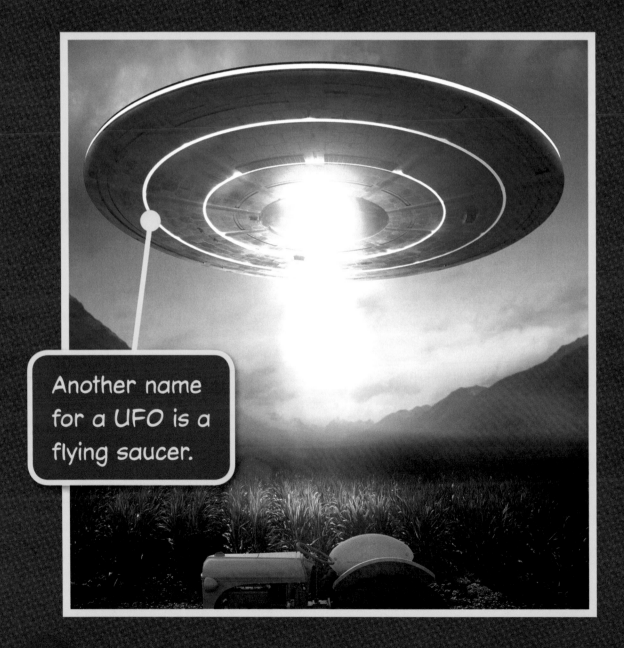

Another name for a UFO is a flying saucer.

Aliens have always been popular in the media.

Alien characters have been in books and movies for more than eighty years. *Star Trek* first aired on TV in 1966. It is about humans, aliens, and space travel.

Early UFO Sightings

On July 4, 1947, a rancher near Roswell, New Mexico, found thin foil pieces in his field. The rancher could not tell what the pieces were. He called the local sheriff.

Disk Craze Continues

Army Disk-ounts New Mexico Find As Weather Gear

FORT WORTH, July 9.—(AP)—An examination by the Army revealed last night that a mysterious object found on a lonely New Mexico ranch was a harmless high-altitude weather balloon—not a grounded flying disk.

Excitement was high in disk-conscious Texas until Brig Gen. Roger M. Ramey, commander of the Eight Air Forces with headquarters here cleared up the mystery.

The bundle of tinfoil, broken wood beams and rubber remnants of a ballon was sent here yesterday by army air transport in the wake of reports that it was a flying disk.

But the general said the objects were the crushed remains of a Ray wind target used to determine the direction and velocity of winds at high altitudes.

Warrant Officer Irving Newton, forecaster at the Army Air Forces weather station here, said "we use them because they go much higher than the eye can see."

LOST PURSE HOLDING DIAMONDS IS FOUND, BUT MONEY MISSING

Somewhere in Corsicana Wed-

NOT A FLYING DISC—Major Jesse A. Marcel of Houma, La., intelligence officer of the 509th Bomb Group at Roswell, New Mexico, inspects what was identified by a Fort Worth, Texas, Army Air Base weather forecaster as a ray wind target used to determine the direction and velocity of winds at high altitudes. Initial stories originating from Roswell, where the object was found, had labelled it a "flying disc" but inspection at Fort Worth revealed its true nature. (AP Wirephoto).

US Air Force soldiers nearby took the pieces back to the base. Some people think the air force was covering up a UFO crash.

In 1955, the air force began using Area 51, a top-secret government site in the Nevada desert. The site is far from towns and cities.

Area 51's official name is the Nevada Test and Training Range at Groom Lake.

Many people say they have seen UFOs around the base. The US government doesn't agree that UFOs are alien spaceships.

TOP SECRET

Many people believe that aliens are in Area 51.

Recent UFO Sightings

In 2006, about a dozen workers at O'Hare International Airport in Chicago, Illinois, say they saw a UFO hover over the airport. It appeared to fly away very fast leaving only a circle in the clouds.

The government explained that weather conditions and airport lights made it look as if a UFO was in the clouds. The government did not look into it any further.

Some people mistake strange but natural-forming clouds as visits from outer space.

One of the most important UFO sightings happened in Phoenix, Arizona, on March 13, 1997. Hundreds of witnesses claimed to have seen a very large V-shaped spaceship.

Someone called the police to look into the strange sight. However, they didn't find anything.

Many people believe that alien spaceships have bright lights on the bottom.

Are UFOs Real?

Have aliens really visited Earth?
No proof of aliens exists,
but no one knows for sure.
Experts can explain mysterious
sightings in many ways.

In 2008, over eight hundred people reported a UFO in Phoenix, Arizona. Two days later, someone admitted to hanging flares from large balloons. Fake events might explain some of the sightings.

Some phone apps will add UFOs to pictures or videos.

Everyday objects can be mistaken for UFOs. Lightning, airplanes, weather balloons, and more can look to some like UFOs.

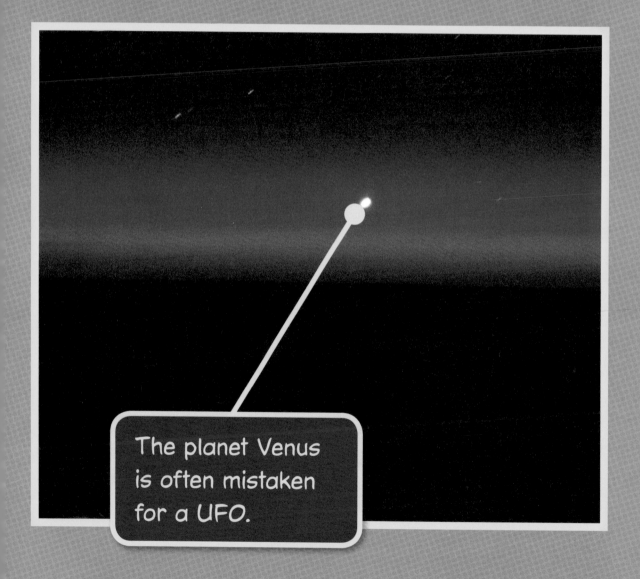

The planet Venus is often mistaken for a UFO.

Our galaxy is very large.
Aliens might live somewhere in
the galaxy, but most people
believe that aliens haven't
visited Earth yet.

Close Encounter

In 1947, pilot Kenneth Arnold saw nine objects flying in the sky over Washington State. Arnold

thought the objects looked like saucers skipping across the water. Newspapers reported Arnold's story wrong. They said he saw flying saucers. Scientists believe Arnold may have seen a flock of pelicans. He might have thought their white feathers looked like lights.

Terrifying Trivia

- Project Blue Book was an air force study of UFOs. It included over twelve thousand reports of sightings from 1952 to 1969.

- Crop circles are large patterns made in fields of wheat or corn by bending the crops over. Some people think that aliens make these circles.

- Scientists use the Drake equation math formula to learn about life on other planets. But scientists disagree on its results.

Glossary

alien: something not from Earth

flare: a bright light shot into the sky to get attention

galaxy: many stars grouped together by scientists to measure distance in space

hover: float in the air in one place

sighting: when someone sees an alien or UFO

spaceship: a vehicle that can travel in space

UFO: unidentified flying object

US Air Force: a branch of the US military

Further Reading

Kenney, Karen Latchana. *Mysterious UFOs and Aliens*. Minneapolis: Lerner Publications, 2018.

Kiddle: "Unidentified Flying Object Facts for Kids" https://kids.kiddle.co/Unidentified_flying_object

National Geographic: "Area 51's Secrets" https://www.nationalgeographic.com.au/tv/area -51s-secrets/

Oachs, Emily Rose. *UFOs*. Minneapolis: Bellwether Media, 2019.

Tieck, Sarah. *Aliens*. Minneapolis: Big Buddy Books, 2016.

Index

Photo Acknowledgments

Image credits: Rastan/Getty Images, p. 2; IgorZh/Shutterstock.com, p. 4; Bettmann/Getty Images, pp. 5, 20; Colin Anderson Productions pty ltd/Getty Images, p. 6; Arun Nevader/Getty Images, p. 7; Marcia Straub/Getty Images, p. 8; Universal History Archive/Getty Images, p. 9; sipaphoto/Getty Images, p. 10; elnavegante/Shutterstock.com, p. 11; carterdayne/Getty Images, p. 12; Denise Taylor/Getty Images, p. 13; cristi180884/Shutterstock.com, p. 14; Fer Gregory/Shutterstock.com, p. 15; koya79/Getty Images, p. 16; Image Source/Getty Images, p. 17; NASA/JSC, p. 18; NASA/JPL, p. 19; koya79/Getty Images, p. 23.

Cover: eugenesergeev/Getty Images (tree), PhonlamaiPhoto/Getty Images (UFO).